THE
POWERSHARING

PEOPLE COMPUTERS AND YOU

SERIES©

A Resource Guide to

The Complete Digital Edition

PROFESSIONALS SHARING KNOWLEDGE

Series Editor: Charles K. Mann, Ph.D.

What is *The Powersharing Series?*

It is a recorded collection of unusually good talks about computers, selected, recorded and edited for this Series. Speakers include computer pioneers telling their stories; industry leaders looking ahead; creators of software explaining their creations. Most talks were recorded at The Boston Computer Society, The Computer Museum, NY user groups. Question and answer sessions enrich most of the presentations. Program length ranges: some 60; most 90; some 120 minutes.

The Powersharing Series was created for:	• Computer professionals who depend upon such informal talks as a key knowledge resource, yet who cannot attend all the best ones in person; Computer company libraries (Microsoft, Borland, Prime).
	• Business people and industry analysts who need to hear the industry leaders but who are not able to attend their talks in person.
	• Educators who understand the learning benefits of hearing the people behind the technology; Students whose portable listening devices become serious learning machines; School, college and university libraries (Stanford, Columbia Teachers, No. Dokata School for the Blind, Pittsburgh Unified Sch. Dist).
	• Computer users who catch on faster to a software program once they hear its creator explain its essence; Public Libraries (Ventura County, Phoenix)
Audio recordings have many advantages:	• They allow people to do two things at once. You can't read and do something else. You can listen and do something else: drive, jog, get dressed, walk to work, rake the leaves, make dinner, ride an exercise bike.
	• Some places where people can read, they may prefer to listen: On the train, on the plane, in the hotel after a long day.
	• Many people prefer to be told about something rather than read about it. Many action-oriented individuals process talk better than text.
	• A speaker has more tools than a writer to get ideas across: inflection, emphasis, volume, pitch, pacing, feedback from audience response.
	• An informal talk conveys a sense of the person speaking. Hearing him or her present ideas and respond to questions in a public forum provides an insight into personality and character. This enriches the context for absorbing knowledge about the technology and the industry.
The Powersharing Series respects you, the listener:	• Powersharing's Editor carefully selects the talks for the Series.
	• The Editor serves as the listeners' man-on-the-spot, providing context for each talk, narrating graphics, explaining mysterious explosions of laughter, keeping the listener in the scene.
	• With the excellent audiences at these talks, the Q&A period often is as important as the talk. Powersharing's powerful "shotgun mike" makes clear all audience questions and comments.
	• Broadcast quality audiocassettes and Dolby noise reduction deliver clear, smooth sound -- especially important when listening with headphones.

Powersharing Series Timeline: 1982 - 2019

1982: Powersharing, Inc. established to co-produce with Emmy Award winner Martha Stuart (PBS: Are You Listening Series) *The Powersharing Series*, a video introduction to using the Apple II and VisiCalc. Introduced to the public at AppleFest82 in Boston and COMDEX 82 in Atlantic City.

1983: Computer Fair in NYC draws many industry pioneers. Powersharing records 30 presentations; selects 11 to begin an audio series: *The Powersharing Series*: *People, Computers and You.*

1985: Recording agreements signed with The Boston Computer Society (monthly meetings and selected special interest group meetings) and The Computer Museum (Pioneers Lecture Series),

1986: Series produced as ring binder collection of 32 audiocassettes supplemented by 24 page Resource Guide.

1989: Second edition of the Resource Guide prepared including descriptions of the 92 programs that then comprised the Series.

1989 - 1991: Mann's work as development economist frequently takes him to Malawi where he serves as Food Policy Advisor. Powersharing continues to record at both the BCS and Computer Museum, videotaping sessions when Mann is out of the country so he can narrate graphics when he edits and produces the programs. Unproduced backlog of recordings grows to 44 programs.

1991: Mann appointed resident economic advisor in The Gambia, followed by four-year assignment in Malawi. Work on *The Powersharing Series* placed on indefinite hold and all recordings and equipment put into in long-term storage.

2002: Mann retires from his Harvard economics career and founds The Development Communications Workshop to mentor students in digital storytelling and produce educational films about international development (distributed by DER.ORG).

2013-2014: Mann resumes work on his "bucket list" goal of completing *The Powersharing Series* and making it widely available. With many eBay purchases of legacy Mac and Aldus/Adobe items, Mann brings all of the 1989 Mac System 7 Powersharing files into a contemporary Mac OSX system for further development; begins work on the recordings themselves.

2015-2019: Facilitated by trustees Gordon Bell and Gardner Hendrie, the Computer History Museum and Powersharing begin a collaboration aimed at completing and digitally publishing the full *Powersharing Series* on the CHM website and permanently archiving all Powersharing materials at CHM. With volunteer editor Tom Frikker, graphic designer Bill Shea, and many others, Mann completes the final digital edition:134 audio programs, 12 videos, 2 mini series, the 24 page *Resource Guide* and index. This Digital Edition is available on a 64GB flash drive at Amazon.com. Information at: www.ThePowersharingSeries.com.

Table of Contents

COMPUTER INDUSTRY

Pgm. No.	Program Title	Speaker	Vignette: Speaker and Talk	Date-Forum
105	**Establishing Market Share in a Worldwide Economy**	Regis McKenna	Fortune calls him "the man who markets Silicon Valley". He presents a critique of U.S. national strategy and proposes ways to improve it.	02/21/1985-Museum
130	**The New Economics of Software**	Adam Osborne	Phoenix-like entrepreneur (Osborne/McGraw-Hill, Osborne Computer) explains concept of Paperback Software, later the target of Lotus lawsuit.	03/03/1985-Museum
106	**Home Computers: An Insider's Guide to the Future**	Trip Hawkins	Visionary President of Electronic Arts sees computer in home as birth of new medium. TV gave window to look thru. Now we can step thru.	06/25/1985-BCS
107	**The Coming Demise of the Personal Computer Industry**	Howard Anderson	Founder and President of Yankee Group; premier market research organization. Especially good on how computers change way firms compete.	11/20/1985-BCS
141	**"Suppose you were IBM . . . "**	Dan Bricklin and Jonathan Rotenberg	When fog prevented the scheduled speaker's appearance, these two staged an impromptu but inspired conversation with The BCS audience.	09/24/1986-BCS
140	**How 1987 will look from 1992**	Howard Anderson	Imaginative and insightful look back from 1992 at 1987 from viewpoint of CEOs of IBM, Apple, DEC. "What we did right; what we did wrong."	11/19/1986-BCS
139	**Impact of the New Electronic Media in the Next Five Years**	Patrick McGovern	Founder of huge publishing empire (ComputerWorld, etc.) draws on his firm's market research to present his vision of the electronic future.	12/11/1986-Museum
142	**Big Chill in the Software Market**	Adam Green	Leading database author gives his and others' views on the Lotus "Look and Feel" lawsuit against Osborne's Paperback Software.	01/21/1987-NYPC
143	**The Battle of the Pundits The BCS' Tenth Birthday**	Alsop, Dvorak, Pournelle, Preston, Seymour	Brilliant analysts all; challenged to make their most outrageous predictions. Kudos to Pournelle for his CD "Library of the Month Club".	02/25/1987-BCS
146	**A Look at the Future**	Jean-Louis Gassée	Author of The Third Apple; Apple VP for Product Development. An engaging talk about personal computers and the cultural revolution.	05/17/1987-Museum
162	**Adam Osborne Predicts . . .**	Adam Osborne	After some remarks about legal profession (but not the suit), presents insightful observations on the major trends he sees shaping the industry.	09/03/1987-BCS-PC
164	**Reflections: Past, Present, Future**	John Sculley	Drawing on insights presented in his book "Odyssey", Apple CEO sketches future of computing. Provocative comments on significance of Hypercard.	10/13/1987-BCS
168	**The Computer Industry in 1995**	Howard Anderson and Michael Goulde	Innovative "point/counter-point" presentation of major trends seen to be shaping the industry towards 1995. "Assume computing power is free."	11/18/1987-BCS
173	**On Technology; To Fulfill the Promise of Personal Computers**	Mitch Kapor	Famous entrepreneur who brought to the world Lotus 1-2-3 shares the vision driving his new firm, On Technology.	02/24/1988-BCS
180	**The "G Word"; Groupware**	Esther Dyson	Publisher of Release 1.0, "Industry's most influential newsletter" (NYT) Insightful overview; approaches to making workgroups more productive.	05/25/1988-BCS
185	**The Future of Personal Computer Operating Systems**	Stewart Alsop II	Ex-BCS'er, now Publisher of PC Letter; top industry newsletter. A look ahead at the operating systems jungle that awaits us.	10/26/1988-BCS

"Dear Dr. Mann,

From the Mailbag:

"...Congratulations on the skill with which you provided the introductory material, as well as the high professional quality of the recording. I was most impressed!"
"You are providing a great service by increasing the availability and the ease of use of the ideas of the world's leading thinkers in the area of information technology. . . ."
Sincerely yours,

Patrick J. McGovern
Chairman of the Board, International Data Group
(Publisher: ComputerWorld, InfoWorld, 106 others)

Listening to Ben Rosen at 32,000 feet.
"Based on our experience, distilling the elements of success, it is clear that
the things that allowed Lotus and Compaq to rise above the others was . . . ."
The Powersharing Series, #114

Pgm. No.	Program Title	Speaker	Vignette: Speaker and Talk	Date-Forum
121	**Artificial Knowledge and the Future of Software**	Esther Dyson	Publisher of Release 1.0; "industry's most influential newsletter" (NY Times); Describes promising "AI" applications; what she sees coming.	02/27/1985-BCS
123	**Where do we want AI to Go?**	Oliver Selfridge	Pioneering AI scientist, now at GTE Labs. Creating software that learns what we want it to do and does it. One of the wisest talks in the Series.	10/27/1985-Museum
124	**Commercializing Artificial Intelligence**	Ray Kurzweil	Founder of Kurzweil Applied Intelligence, Inc. Good talk about AI, mind-blowing demos: Kurzweil music system; voice controlled DB, WP.	02/26/1986-BCS
138	**Using Computers to Help People Think for Themselves**	Timothy Leary	Popular Psychologist and entrepreneur behind "Mind Mirror", trail-blazing "thought processor". New horizons in thinking independently.	10/22/1986-BCS
136	**Human Intelligence and The Future of Computers**	Marvin Minsky	Co-founder, Artificial Intelligence Lab, M.I.T.; author "The Society of Mind"; superb informal supplement to this landmark book.	12/17/1986-BCS
135	**The Age of Intelligent Machines**	Ray Kurzweil Edward Feigenbaum George Gilder	Founder of Kurzweil Applied Intelligence, Inc. His soundtrack for Museum of Science Film is part of this program. Chairman, Computer Science Dept. Stanford Univ.; AI Pioneer. Noted author, "Wealth and Poverty"; astute observer of information age.	01/28/1987-BCS
170	**Kurzweil's Amazing Machines**	Ray Kurzweil	Explanations and impressive demos: reading machine; text entry by scanning; voice entry expert systems, dazzling music system..	12/16/1987-BCS

Sharing Power

Over three centuries ago, Francis Bacon wrote "Knowledge itself is power". Even truer now than then, the personal computer lies at the heart of today's knowledge explosion. It has given millions of people new access to knowledge, new personal and professional productivity, new power to analyze more insightfully, to write more forcefully, to communicate more widely and richly, to learn more efficiently. Unlike other sorts of power, knowledge expands through sharing. Recognizing this, some of the most creative spirits and gifted participants in the computer revolution enthusiastically share with others their knowledge through informal talks.

Sharing Knowledge

As a example of a rich learning environment, MIT Professor Seymour Papert, father of LOGO, points to Brazil's Samba Clubs. There is a great resemblance between the stimulating yet supportive environment he describes and that of today's computer user groups. Suffusing this environment is the spirit of sharing which characterizes the computer community at its best and most exhilarating. *The Powersharing Series* helps to extend the reach of such sharing by capturing and distributing important informal talks. These convey both knowledge and a sense of the enthusiasms and personalities that animate the industry. In cooperation with the speakers themselves and the talks' organizers, the Series both preserves and multiplies the usefulness of their insights. It represents a potent knowledge resource.

"For those of you who commute, these tapes are good alternatives to specialized news and talk shows. A regular subscription to the tapes can provide members with an "All Things Considered on Computing."

Dr. Gwen K. Bell, Founding President, The Computer Museum

The Director's Letter, Spring, 1985

The Independent Learner

Many of the people who use the personal computer to make their personal and professional lives more productive have developed learning strategies to make themselves independent learners. They draw upon a variety of informal information resources. They develop frameworks which help them integrate and assimilate information from all these diverse sources. Many have learned to use effectively the informal educational resources of such organizations as The Boston Computer Society, computer user groups, and The Computer Museum. The learning style particularly appropriate to these informal learning environments has been called "sticky paper learning".

COMPUTER SYSTEMS

Pgm. No.	Program Title	Speaker	Vignette: Speaker and Talk	Date- Forum
110	The Atari ST Computer	Leonard Tramiel, Bruce Cohen, William Bowman	Legendary Jack's son (Atari's VP Software Dev.) introduces ST. Digital Research's Cohen describes GEM op. sys. Spinnaker's Chmn. Bowman sees start of new era of graphic programming, requiring new mindsets.	03/27/1985-BCS
109	Commodore Presents Amiga!	Tom Rattigan, Adam Chowaniec, Robert Pariseau	CEO of Commodore, VP Technology, VP Software give design principles and market strategy of then new Amiga. Pariseau rich in technical detail of special interest to developers.	08/28/1985-BCS
111	The Present and Future of Macintosh	Del Yocam	Apple's Exec. VP introduces the Mac Plus and discusses principles of Mac development philosophy. Musical intro alone is a collector's item.	01/22/1986-BCS
145	The Amiga 500 and Amiga 2000	Tom Rattigan and Henri Rubin	CEO and design team put impressive new models through their paces. Insights into design concepts for current or prospective Amiga users.	03/25/1987-BCS
147	The Macintosh SE and Macintosh II	Charlie Oppenheimer and Didier Diaz	Project managers of SE and II orchestrate spectacular introduction to enthusiastic audience of 1500. Q&A is a rich resource info for Mac users.	03/27/1987-BCS-MAC
149	The IBM Personal System/2	Bill Machrone	Following IBM's presentation of its new PS/2 line, respected Editor of PC Magazine assesses significance of new architecture. Excellent Q&A.	05/07/1987-BCS-PC
155	Netstations for Workgroup Computing	Bob Metcalfe	Inventor of Ethernet and founder of 3Com makes persuasive case for people working in groups to use diskless netstations with common fileserver. Impressively easy set-up and connections.	05/28/1987-BCS
150	Future Developments in Personal Computers (Part One: Talk)	Bill Gates	Co-founder of Microsoft and computer legend assays the future of personal computing and explains new language products.	06/03/1987-BCS
151	Future Developments in Personal Computers (Part Two: Q&A)	Bill Gates	Extensive technical Q&A session with Gates; not for the novice, but a treasure trove of information for developers.	06/03/1987-BCS
156	The Connection Machine	John Mucci	VP of Thinking Machines Corp. presents principles of massive parallel processing (65,000 microprocessors) and suggests new ways of thinking about graphics, image and text processing, simulations and database.	06/24/1987-BCS
144	Tandy's Challenge to IBM	John Roach	CEO of Tandy Corp. introduces formidable new line of Radio Shack computers competing head-to-head with IBM.	09/30/1987-BCS
172	What is OS/2, Anyway?	Camenker, Machrone, Belove, Tarter	BCS'er explains OS/2 "so an 8 year old can understand it." Judgements by Editor of PC Magazine; top Lotus scientist; newsletter publisher.	01/07/1988-BCS-PC
175	The Future of Macintosh	Bill Gates	The co-founder and CEO of Microsoft tells the story of the Macintosh, past and future, just before Apple hit Microsoft with the famous lawsuit.	02/08/1988-BCS-MIT
174	The Future of IBM's PS/2 and OS/2	Bill Lowe	The head of IBM's entire personal computer operation looks ahead; fields the tough questions of a sophisticated BCS audience.	03/23/1988-BCS
181	Microsoft's CD-ROM	Carl Stork	Microsoft's Director of CD-ROM Marketing shows the power that it puts in the hands of writers, small business, market researchers.	04/02/1988-BCS-PC
179	PC's Limited; The Dell Computer Company	Michael Dell	From mail order in a college dorm to a major new force in the computer industry, all by age 26. Powerful new computers; innovative marketing.	04/27/1988-BCS
186	UNIX: Past, Present, Future	Dennis Ritchie	Insights from the co-creator (with long-time collaborator Ken Thompson) of the UNIX operating system and creator of "C" language.	05/01/1988-Museum
183	Sir Clive Sinclair's Briefcase Computer	Nigel Searle	From the man who brought us the handheld calculator and the Sinclair portable; low cost, true desktop power to slip into your briefcase.	06/22/1988-BCS
184	CDI: Compact Disk Interactive DVI: Digital Video Interactive	Linda Helgerson and Holly Faubel	Publisher, leading CD-ROM newsletter provides overview; HF on DVI applications, ending with the demo that blew them away at Microsoft.	08/24/1988-BCS
189	Compaq's New Laptop	Rod Canion	CEO and co-founder of Compaq shares stories of Compaq's early years and demonstrates features of Compaq's newest laptop.	10/18/1989-NYPC

Sticky-Paper Learning

Sticky-paper learning is an allusion to the old-fashioned fly paper which once hung in the kitchen to catch flies. It was incredibly sticky stuff that pulled out of a roll and hung down from the ceiling like a New Year's Eve streamer. It attracted flies. Once they alighted, they never got off. The mind of the independent learner is like that. It attracts information and holds it.

To get the most out of *The Powersharing Series* it is useful to know about sticky-paper learning. Otherwise, the lack of formal structure in the talks may be frustrating. Particularly for the newcomer to a topic, there are many mystery terms and concepts. However, the very frustration of not knowing all the terms serves to make the paper even stickier. The sticky-paper learner begins actively to read, ask and listen for explanations: becomes an active agent in the learning process.

Computer Group Networks

In the context of sticky paper learning, computer groups are especially powerful learning environments for at least two reasons. First, some member of the group can and will explain almost anything you want to know about computers. Secondly, the talks presented there will keep your head full of new terms and concepts which will enlarge the size and scope of your mental sticky paper. You begin to trap information about these new concepts from your reading, from asking people questions, from hearing more talks which put the terms in a richer context.

Gradually you begin to be able to see things in categories; you begin to form a framework for your knowledge which in turn facilitates deeper understandings. Some talks and articles explicitly try to help build such structures of knowledge. These are especially helpful in integrating previously unrelated fragments on your sticky paper. Increasingly you begin to see things within a broader context and hence to understand them more fully.

SOFTWARE: THE CREATORS' PERSPECTIVE

Pgm. No.	Program Title	Speaker	Vignette: Speaker and Talk	Date-Forum
129	Computers and New Ways of Thinking Focus on TK Solver	Robert Frankston	Co-creator of VisiCalc. Insights on how computers change the way we think about problems. Frankston illustrates with then new TK Solver!.	09/24/1983-NY Fair
131	Computer Control of the Home	Reuel O. Launey	Because this talk presents the basic principles and rationale of a home control system, it serves as an excellent introduction to the subject. Launey is the creator of the home control software Waldo.	09/24/1983-NY Fair
113	Selecting a Database Management System	Adam Green	Leading database author and teacher. Clear and concise presentation of a framework for thinking about database management programs.	09/24/1983-NY Fair
122	Software Superstars!	Terrence Garnett Adam Bosworth Philippe Kahn	Creator of Lightyear, interactive decision aid program noted by Dyson. Creator of Reflex presents concepts underlying this database program. Borland's founder. Bought Reflex; dropped its price from $495 to $99. Demos new SuperKey.	04/25/1985-BCS
114	ANSA's Paradox Explained	Benjamin M. Rosen Stephen Dow	World's premier venture capitalist (Compaq, Lotus, ANSA). Insights into both VC and expectations for Paradox. Dow and creators demonstrate.	09/25/1985-BCS
112	New Directions in Software	Tom Snyder	With his software, strives to create "rich, deep, symbolic environment that begs kids or adults to explore". Includes a hilarious spoof BogusSoft Ed.	10/23/1985-BCS
115	Software Breakthroughs: Javelin; Q&A; Framework II	S. Kugel, C. Herot V.Rayburn, G. Hendricks Robert Carr	Co-creator of Javelin presents concepts underlying ten view spreadsheet. Pres. of Symantec and creator of Q&A explain AI assisted database pgm. Creator of this word processor-spreadsheet combo explains its concepts.	12/18/1985-BCS
108	What Comes After the Personal Computer?	Jef Raskin	"The man who invented the Macintosh" presents his vision of the future of personal computing; demonstrates his Swyftware. Marvelously entertaining talk.	03/26/1986-BCS
116	Lotus HAL Explained	Ezra Gottheil Bill and Larry Gross Alexis Driscoll	Product manager for HAL, productivity tool for Lotus 1-2-3. Creators of HAL present concepts and narrate demonstration. Product Marketing Manager for HAL explains marketing strategy.	04/23/1986-BCS
154	MathCAD Explained Alpha/three Explained	David Blum Selwyn Rabins	Creator of MathCAD, the engineer's scratchpad, explains program concepts. One of creators of Alpha/three: builds on the DBase III standard.	06/25/1986-BCS
148	Superstar II: Sprint Word Processor Explained	Philippe Kahn	Founder of Borland International; called by Wall Street Journal "L'enfant terrible of Silicon Valley". Explains dazzling word processor.	04/22/1987-BCS
163	The New Generation of Databases	Bert Collins	The head of the BCS-PC Database Group provides a framework to help understand the new databases. Excellent!	10/01/1987-BCS-PC
165	Understanding Hypercard	Bill Atkinson	Creator of Hypercard (and MacPaint), Atkinson holds the audience spellbound as he shares his visions of this seminal software. Don't settle for second-hand descriptions of Hypercard.	11/04/1987-NYMUG
169	The New 1-2-3 and Agenda	Jim Manzi, Mitch Kapor, Lotus Product Managers	Lotus Chairman Manzi looks ahead; "Intro" of Release 3.0; Kapor explains concepts underlying his Agenda; its author narrates demonstration.	12/13/1987-BCS-PC
171	The Borland Way: Quattro and Sidekick Plus	Philippe Kahn	Borland's brilliant and flamboyant founder demonstrates Quattro's innovative features, positioning it to challenge 1-2-3's dominant S/S lead. He also shows off the new features of Sidekick Plus.	01/27/1988-BCS

Computer Groups Know the Good Speakers

Central to the rich learning environment of the various computer groups is their ability to tap the knowledge, enthusiasm and explanatory skills of leading personalities in the field. Moreover, they can recognize within their own membership those with exceptional gifts in explaining various topics to others. In a well-presented, lively talk the personality of the speaker suffuses, enlivens and invigorates the information itself. It helps add stickiness to the paper. Hearing many speakers gradually builds up a sense of the personalities behind the technology. This adds contextual richness to the learning process, making it more engaging and hence more effective.

This sticky paper learning goes on all the time within the networks of the computer user community. It is not neat and orderly the way a formal educator would want it. It is messy; always incomplete, often frustrating. But over time, it is a powerful and highly cumulative learning process.

Who is listening to *The Powersharing Series*?

"The Powersharing Series . . . . plus a Walkman, portable cassette player or built-in car stereo cassette player can help turn housework, jogging, pedaling the exercise bicycle, or driving through rush-hour gridlock . . . into productive learning time."

Gail Thomas, Synapse
(Connected Education Newsletter)

"Thanks for the tapes which arrived in good order!
They're my only 'live' connection with the computer world."
Listener in The Gambia, West Africa

EDUCATION AND GAMES

Pgm. No.	Program Title	Speaker	Vignette: Speaker and Talk	Date-Forum
125	**Computers and the Future of Schooling**	Seymour Papert	MIT's Father of Logo makes persuasive case for new learning environments to serve diverse learning styles: "sculptors" as well as "planners."	09/24/1983-NY Fair
128	**Integrating Computers into the Elementary School Curriculum & Writing Workshops Using Computers**	Alice-Anne Winner, Jeanne Forester, Peggy O'Brien	Three teachers at the United Nations International School give insights on use of word processing in teaching writing; framework for thinking about role of computers in schools; writing program for English as a foreign language.	09/24/1983-NY Fair
126	**Educational Excellence through Home/ School Cooperation**	Kenneth Komoski	Prof, Teachers College, Columbia U. and Pres. EPIE (Educational Products Info. Exchange): Sets forth fears, dreams, recommendations for equity and effectiveness of computers in schools.	09/24/1983-NY Fair
137	**Computers and Learning in Early Childhood**	Seymour Papert	Describes experimental computer classrooms where the ideas set forth in Future of Schooling are being put into practice. Includes Leggo-Logo.	04/17/1986-Museum
157	**What Works: Implementation Ideas & Science, Technology and Fate Control**	Bobby Goodson Adeline Naiman	For California School System, scoured the state for exemplary uses of classroom computers. Columnist for Computer Update: engaging talk on promise and pitfalls.	05/11/1987-Lesley College
153	**Connected Education: Computer Teleconferencing for Credit**	Paul Levinson and Tina Vozick	The Founders of Connected Education, Inc. describe how and why to take college courses by teleconference. (New School for Social Research)	05/15/1987-ConnEd
176	**The Past of Computer Games**	David Ahl Ken Arnold Steve Russell	Editor of *Basic Computer Games* and founder of *Creative Computing*. Creators of *Rogue* and *Spacewar!* discuss the evolution of computer games for both recreation and education..	11/07/1987-Museum
177	**The Future of Computer Games (Part One)**	Dave Lebling Chris Crawford Tom Snyder	Wonderful talks on games, computers and people by the creators of Zork (Lebling), Balance of Power (Crawford), Puppy Love (Snyder), 7 Cities of Gold (Bunten). Scientific American's Dewdney is Moderator.	11/07/1987-Museum
178	**The Futute of Computer Games (Part Two)**	Dan Bunten, A.K. Dewdney	Game program continuation: includes freewheeling discussion panelists and knowledgeable audience (including game reviewer Roe Adams)..	11/07/1987-Museum
187	**Classware for Teachers ; Lapware for Parents**	Tom Snyder David Dockterman	Educational software pioneers presents wise and funny multimedia evening. Match wits with BCS audience in ID of quotes; Hear BCS child rewrite classic fairy tale with Syder's lapware.	09/28/1988-BCS
188	**Technology as a Catalyst for Restructuring Schools**	Alan November	One of five educators in the nation awarded the Christa McAuliffe Award; President of Mass. Computer Using Educators. Hard look at what computers cannot do; why and how to restructure schools. Excellent!	10/12/1988-BCS-Ed

---

Dear Dr. Mann:

From one Steve Wozniak fan club member to another, we do wish to thank you for the marvelous collection of Powersharing Tapes. Students and I have enjoyed listening to them and certainly have learned and profited from your generous gift.

We wish you continued success with the Powersharing Series.

> *Sincerely yours,*
> *Gert Abery, Teacher*
> *Annie Fisher School, Hartford, CT*

(CKM sent some Steve Wozniak tapes to her students who are his "pen pals".)

From the Mailbag:

"I touch the future. I teach."
> *Christa McAuliffe*

On the board in his Wellesley Middle School classroom as Alan November begins his talk to The BCS Education group. Christa McAuliffe was a teacher from Concord NH and was one of the seven crew members killed in the Space Shuttle Challenger explosion on January 28, 1986.

David Ahl opening the Games Symposium: From
The Powersharing Series, #176

"I don't have a blackboard, so I'd like you to visualize . . . a Venn diagram with three overlapping circles. The one at the top is **Games** -- that's this big one; then this one over here is **Puzzles**; and this one over here which overlaps the other two is **Simulations**, and I think there is a great overlap between these three separate fields. Simulations can be very serious: a simulation of a military movement; of a satellite; of the travelling salesman problem.

Puzzles can also be very serious; some of them can be scientific puzzles; others can be just sort of 'brain-teaser' puzzles. Games we know can take a wide range: fantasy games to 'shoot-em-up' spacewar* games to Pacman type of games. But, one of the journalists last night asked me, 'What makes a good computer game? 'What's a classic game? Why, for example, is Spacewar still played, why is it still revered?

'Here, let's go back to those three overlapping circles. I think its a game that kind of falls in the middle -- that has some elements of gaming: fantasy, fun, all of these things that we associate with games; and it has some elements of simulations -- simulation of the real world. If it's totally fantasy, I think that kind of limits it.

There's a realm of totally fantasy games, but if you have some elements of the real world, of simulation, of real-world processes, of real people, then there's a hook that the person - the player - can grab onto, can relate to. And it should have some element of puzzlement; solving a puzzle. That's why some of the Infocom games are so good; because you've got the fantasy, you've got the hook to the real world, the simulation aspect of it; and the solving of puzzles. And they will be classic games, as will be some of the others.

If you think of those computer games which have stood the test of time so far . . . they have elements of many, many different layers of interest, of challenge, and they touch on these [three] different areas.

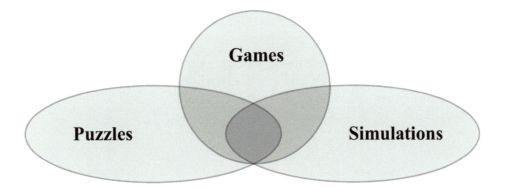

*Martin Graetz and Alan Kotok describe the origins of the original Spacewar game in *The Powersharing Series*, #101

Pgm. No.	Program Title	Speaker	Vignette: Speaker and Talk	Date-Forum
166	**The Future of Personal Computers as seen on October 15, 1981 (Part 1)**	James Finke Bill Gates Peter Rosenthal Jon Shirley	Landmark BCS panel, moderated by Jonathan Rotenberg. In order: CEO Commodore CEO Microsoft Dir. Business Planning Atari VP Computer Merchandising Tandy	10/15/1981-BCS
167	**The Future of Personal Computers as seen on October 15, 1981 (Part 2)**	A.C. Mike Markkula Philip Don Estridge Nigel Searle	CEO Apple Creator of IBM PC Exec.VP Sinclair Original recording by *Creative Computing*; provided for *The Powersharing Series* by CC founder, David Ahl	10/15/1981-BCS
100	**Keynote: The Past and Future of Apple Computer**	Steve Jobs and Steve Wozniak	"Insightful picture of where Apple has been; how its philosophies are evolving and how it plans to move in the coming years." AppleFest Pgm. Jobs' response to questions foreshadows Macintosh interface.	05/15/1982-AppleFest Boston
103	**An Oral History of Apple Computer**	Steve Wozniak	While there is some overlap with #133, Woz was still with Apple at this time. More information about company origins, persona and philosophy.	09/24/1983-NY Fair
127	**The Making of the Bank Street Writer**	D. Midian Kurland	Member of Bank Street College's design team describes conception and pedagogy underlying now famous classroom word processor.	09/24/1983-NY Fair
101	**Spacewar! The Making of the First Computer Game**	Martin Graetz and Alan Kotok	Two early MIT "hackers" whose "play" led to computer breakthroughs. Fascinating insights into the nature of the creative process.	02/24/1985-Museum
104	**The Story of VisiCalc**	Dan Bricklin	As Harvard Business School student, dreamed of a "magic spreadsheet". With Bob Frankston, turned it into the reality of VisiCalc. The rise, the collapse; a new start with Dan Bricklin's Demo Program.	09/17/1985-NYPC
191	**The Origins of the Personal Computer**	Alan Kay	Superb oral history of early developments, especially at Xerox PARC: graphical user interface, the mouse, windows. As with all Powersharing programs, Editor Mann describes Kay's many graphics. Not yet released.	10/13/1985-Museum
102	**Microcomputers: Looking Back, Looking Ahead**	Les Solomon	Wonderful stories from the retired Popular Electronics editor whose 1975 Altair cover story now stands as marking the start of the PC era.	04/16/1986-NYPC
133	**The Making of an Engineer and a Computer**	Steve Wozniak	Authentic American folk hero, creator of the enduring Apple II, spins a beautiful tale of adventure and discovery. In school resource centers, helps young users see computer in a context they can relate to.	05/13/1986-Museum
134	**The Pioneers of Personal Computers**	John Blankenbaker Thi Trong Ed Roberts Lee Felsenstein	The stories of creators of (in order): the earliest personal computer (Kenbak 1); the first commercially successful one (Micral); opener of PC era (Altair); memory mapped video display, Sol and Osborne computers.	06/14/1986-Museum
159	**The Role of Government and University in Computer Development**	Erich Bloch	The Director of the National Science Foundation examines the forces driving innovation in the computer industry.	06/15/1986-Museum
190	**Boston Debut of NeXT at Boston's Symphony Hall. Includes NeXT music.**	Steve Jobs	Jobs introduces NeXT. According to Wikipedia, "A NeXT Computer and its object oriented development tools and libraries were used by Tim Berners-Lee and Robert Cailliau to develop ... the WorldWideWeb."	11/30/1988-BCS

Bill Gates: From *The Powersharing Series*, #166

"I spent three years in Cambridge going to school.

Microsoft actually got its beginning when my partner came in with a magazine when I was losing at an all-night poker game and showed me the Altair computer on the cover*. I quickly cashed out my chips and went out and read the article about the first general purpose microcomputer, and so it's actually just in this area that we did our first work and wrote the 8080 microcomputer BASIC."
BCS, October 15, 1981

* Les Solomon, the man behind the landmark *Popular Electronics* Altair cover story, provides his first-hand perspective on that seminal story in *The Powersharing Series* #102

Personalities and Context

Better than the written word, recordings of talks to live audiences help to capture a sense of the individual personality. Telling of his dream for a computer of his very own, Steve Wozniak captivates the audience with his excitement and enthusiasm. The dynamism of the personality behind the ubiquitous Apple II can enrich the context for learning for the millions of children who daily sit before the progeny of Wozniak's enduring creation.

Don Estridge: From *The Powersharing Series*, #167

"I've been wanting to participate personally with personal computers ever since the day that Popular Electronics published its issue with the Altair on the cover. [*Powersharing #102*] I wasn't playing poker. My wife and I had other obligations. . ."

I believe . . . history will record that we as individuals and we collectively as a society owe a debt to the pioneers in the field of personal computing, some of whom are here at the table with me, some who have recently appeared on the cover of popular magazines. They earned that reputation by the school of hard knocks and at great personal risk.

Without trying to be too corny, just as our forefathers blazed the trail to the west, these pioneers blazed a new trail, one of personal curiosity, personal creativity, and personal productivity and they found a new pot of gold, which was our individual minds and how to apply them. I don't think any tool, any machine, has come along which lets anyone apply their mind to a greater extent than the personal computer."

BCS, October 15, 1981: 64 days after the introduction of his creation, the IBM PC.

On August 2, 1985, Philip Don Estridge died in the crash of Delta Flt 191 in Dallas, Texas.

COMMUNICATIONS AND NETWORKING

Pgm. No.	Program	Speaker	Vignette: Speaker and Talk	Date-Forum
117	**The World of Computer Communication**	Neil Shapiro	Pathbreaking "Sysop" of one of the earliest electronic computer user groups (MAUG); author & editor. Classic introduction to this topic.	09/24/1983-NY Fair
118	**Understanding Computer Communication**	Joseph Vanginderen	IBM computer scientist and longtime member NYC user groups. Clear introduction to key concepts in modem communications.	09/24/1983-NY Fair
119	**WATSON! Interactive Voice Technology**	Charles Foskett	CEO, Natural Microsystems; system's creators explain and demonstrate how Watson in a PC can make the telephone work harder and longer.	05/22/1985-Museum
120	**DECTALK: Principles & Uses of Computer Synthesized Speech**	Walt Techner Dennis Klatt	The man who brought Klatt's invention to DEC. Q&A including Gordon Bell. Pioneer in speech synthesis at MIT and creator of DECTALK. Includes excellent presentation of principles of computer speech synthesis. Recording includes DECTALK talking.	09/29/1985-Museum
161	**Social Impacts of Computer Conferencing**	Paul Levinson	Co-founder, Connected Education, Inc. Plenary speech at Second Guelph Conference; one of the pioneers in educational computer conferencing.	06/01/1987-Univ.Guelph

YOUR OWN BUSINESS // THE ELECTRONIC COTTAGE

Pgm. No.	Program Title	Speaker	Vignette: Speaker and Talk	Date-Forum
160	**How to Start and Survive in Business with your Personal Computer**	F.L.Mike Harvey	Founder and Publisher of Nibble magazine shares lessons of experience in this classic statement of basic principles and enduringly good advice..	05/16/1982-AppleFest - Boston
152	**Marketing Shareware**	Jim Button Tom Smith Marshall Magee	The originator of the concept of shareware (PC File) explains its origins and principles; shareware stars tell their stories (Procomm, Automenu)	07/02/1987-BCS-PC
182	**Working at Home**	Mike Rohrbach Catherine Marenghi Joan Sweeney	Landmark founding of a new BCS SubGroup; Rohrbach runs large business from his house Marenghi works at home in Boston for a large NYC firm Sweeney at home is a key figure in national networking firm.	04/13/1988-BCS-Soc. Impact

INTERNATIONAL

Pgm. No.	Program Title	Speaker	Vignette: Speaker and Talk	Date-Forum
132	**Computers in the Third World**	Bruce Vogeli and Charles Mann	Columbia University Prof. sees beneficial potentials of computers in Third World, but has deep concern about possibility for polarization haves/havenots. Development economist Mann contrasts outcomes of two Tunisian installations.	09/24/1983-NY Fair
158	**Personal Computers in Developing Countries**	Alex Randall and Clay Wescott	Randall shares the personal computer overview he gave as Fulbright lecturer in Turkey and Ethiopia, plus feedback he got there. Wescott describes computerization of Kenyan national budget that he assisted.	05/04/1987-BCS Internat.

Online Publishing in the news:

"McGraw-Hill says BIX has more than 25,000 subscribers and will become profitable next year. . . . BIX users have seen their electronic musings find their way into print in BYTE, in a section called 'Best of BIX'. Not long ago BYTE editors wandering through BIX were struck by insightful comments on telecommunications from a subscriber in San Diego. Today, the subscriber, Brock Meeks, is a regular BYTE contributor, one of several the magazine has recruited from BIX."

Michael W. Miller, Wall Street Journal, October 19, 1988

Planners, Sculptors, and *The Powersharing Series*

In one of the first talks produced in *The Powersharing Series*, Professor Seymour Papert speaks about different learning styles. He talks of the Planners and the Sculptors.

The Powersharing Series is more for the Sculptors — those who can tolerate some ambiguity and loose ends in their learning; those who do not need to have everything explicitly laid out in well-orchestrated modules. These are the Independent Learners; the persons who are prepared to accept some messiness in the learning process, because they themselves take charge of integrating new knowledge with what they already know.

The unresolved loose ends form more sticky paper for future knowledge capture. Moreover, there is an excitement in receiving knowledge firsthand from the real leaders in the field; knowledge they share enthusiastically with audiences who want to know. If you couldn't be there in person, be there with *The Powersharing Series*.

WITH THE ELECTRONIC NETWORKING ASSOCIATION: TWO MINI-SERIES

1988 - Beyond Electronic Mail

1989 - Groupware: The Next Wave -a Network of People

These edited audiocassettes present selected sessions from two extraordinary Annual Conferences of the young and exuberant ENA at the dawn of the Internet era. They capture the richness of the worlds of computer conferencing, online publishing, online databases, and electronic democracy. They convey a sense of the remarkable personalities behind this electronic trailblazing, as ENA speakers share their ideas, visions, hopes, fears, disasters and triumphs.

Electronic Networking Association Annual Conference, May 1988
"Beyond Electronic Mail" Eight Audiocassette Mini-series

ENA #1	Information Frontier v. Comm. Highways Global Messaging;The Global Village is Here	Art Kleiner Bill Louden	Co-Editor, Whole Earth Software Catalog; author, Mirror on Desktop General Manager of GEnie, part of General Electric's Info. Services
ENA #2	The Power of Computer Conferencing Personal Computing: Has it met the Promise? The Business Future	Mike Greenly Alfred Glossbrenner Phil Moore	Standing ovation for this talk by this pioneering electronic journalist. Author, How to look it up Online; many sessions refer back to this talk. Pres. Networking and World Information (NWI); ex IBM'er (cont. on #3)
ENA #3A	Potholes in the Highways of the Mind	Dave Hughes,Bob Shayon	Pioneering Sysop, proprietor of online "Roger's Bar" + U. Penn Prof.
ENA #3B	Global Boundary Bashing	International Networkers	Strategies for transcending international barriers; Chaotic cafe setting reminded your editor of the galactic bar scene in Starwars.
ENA #4	Interactive Online Publishing: Potentials and Pitfalls (All-day session)	George Bond Charles Bowen Paul Gillin	Executive Editor, BIX Author, Editor, Compuserve's Online Today Executive Editor, Computerworld
ENA #5	What is it and who is doing it? What are the issues for service providers?	Mike Greenly Stefanie Kott Rich Malloy	Pioneering online journalist and marketing consultant DesKott Publishing Associate Managing Editor, News and Technology, BYTE
ENA #6A	What are the issues for the users?	"Dusty" Miller Ed Yarrish	TrainingPlus, facilitator Managing Associate, Executive Technology
ENA #6B	Electronic Democracy: France's Minitel	Don Straus || David Lytel	Moderator: Ex-Pres.Amer. Arbitration Found. || Researcher on Minitel
ENA #7	Getting it together in a political campaign Bringing the world to the rural schoolhouse Computer communications & political power	Andrew Konstantaras Frank and Regina Odasz Dave Hughes	Computer Communications Coordinator, Simon for President Campaign Big Sky Telegraph; innovative online resources for teachers Chariot; harnessing computer conferencing to democracy
ENA #8A	Information Service Futures:Online Databases Common gateways; AudioTex, VideoTex	Walsh; Green;Weinberger Rubinyi; Richards	Ex-Mg. Ed.&Mgr. Publishing Serv, The Source; Dialog Info Services; Telebase (EasyNet); Ext. Serv., U. Minn.; VideoTex Indus Assoc.
ENA #8B	International Networking	Jim Morgan;Noreen Janus	VP & Exec Dir, Rodale Inst & Chrmn, CARINET; Exec Dir CARINET

Electronic Networking Association Annual Conference, May 1989
"Groupware: The Next Wave - a Network of People" Fifteen Audiocassette Mini-series

Opening Panel: Looking Back 10 Years and Forward to Where this Concept is Leading Us	Conferencing by Lawyers: State of the Art; Alternatives; the Future
What's Happening in this World of Ours - and Theirs?	The Risks and the Potential Legal Liability
The Global Classroom: Kids Network	Dispute Resolution using Teleconferencing
The Global Classroom: The (Coming) Global Electronic University	Networking and the Mass Media
The Global Classroom: Electronic Networks for Interaction: ENFI	Beyond Linear Life Stages - Rethinking Life-long Learning
The Global Classroom: Faxon Linx	Connection with Heart of Matters in a Virtual Learning Community
Online Degree Programs	Report from Japan, The Soviet Connection

WHO SPONSORED THE TALKS?

Co-Founder and President of the Boston Computer Society, Jonathan Rotenberg. opens a meeting.

Evenings With The Boston Computer Society

Founded in 1977, the BCS is a non-profit organization whose goal is to help people understand and use personal computers in their personal and professional lives. The highlights are the General Meetings, hosted by BCS President Jonathan Rotenberg (at left). These feature informal talks by leaders and innovators in the industry. Virtually every leading authority on personal computers from around the world has been a guest speaker at a BCS General Meeting. Their talks chronicle the growth of the nation's most dynamic industry. They contain not only useful information about products and trends in the industry, but fascinating insights on the evolving role of the computer in business, education and home. With worldwide membership peaking at 31,100 in June, 1989, membership began to decline with the rise of the Internet and other information sources. In September 1996, the BCS Board declared "Mission Accomplished" and unanimously voted to disband the 18,000 member organization.

The Computer Museum

With their personal collection as the nucleus, in 1979, Gordon and Gwen Bell founded the Digital Computer Museum in Marlboro MA. In 1983, the "Digital" was dropped and the Computer Museum moved to Museum Wharf in Boston. It was the world's only museum dedicated to preserving the past, present, and future of computers. In addition to many exhibits and a permanent gallery featuring history, technology, and applications, the Museum sponsored a series of "Pioneer Lectures" and Powersharing recorded many of these for *the Powersharing Series*. In 1996, the Museum Board established in Silicon Valley a Computer History Division that was soon expanded to become the Computer History Museum. In 1999, the Computer Museum merged with Boston's Museum of Science, sending much of its historical collection to the new Computer History Museum.

President and Co-Founder (with husband and computer pioneer Gordon Bell) of The Computer Museum.

BAUG NYPC UNIS **The New York Computer Fair**

Periodically computer user groups join together to produce truly remarkable educational events. One such event was the 1983 Computer Fair in New York sponsored by the Big Apple User's Group (BAUG), New York Personal Computer, Inc. (NYPC), and the United Nations International School (UNIS). The web of member contacts drew to this Fair an extraordinary group of speakers including Apple II designer Steve Wozniak. Powersharing recorded thirty-two presentations there. Eleven were selected for the Series as exceptionally good and of enduring interest. The New York groups continue to sponsor excellent talks, some of which are included in the Series, such as Dan Bricklin (VisiCalc co-creator) and Les Solomon (*Popular Electronics* Altair cover story) at the NYPC and Bill Atkinson (MacPaint, Hypercard) at the New York Macintosh Users Group.

PROGRAMS PRODUCED 2015-2019

Category	Forum	Date	Speaker	Program Title and Information	Pgm. No.
Computer Industry	BCS-GM	8/23/89	Stewart Alsop II	Newsletter Guru: *25 Predictions.* Sees NeXT as model for other computers.	217
	BCS-GM	12/20/89	SIGGRAPH w Chris Herot	Software leader narrates *New Developments in Computer Graphics.*	222
	BCS-SI	3/13/85	BCS Panel including Pres. Rotenberg	Discussion of *The Mission of BCS Social Impact Group* and the changing role of the BCS.	192
	BCS-SI	6/12/85	Richard Stallman and Marvin Goldschmidt	Open source advocate and Lotus Exec.: *Debate: Copyright v. Copy Protection*.	196
	Harvard IT Series	3/6/85	Akio Morita	Co-founder Sony Corp.: Includes reflections on Japanese v. American culture and business philosophy.	194
	Harvard IT Series	2/1/89	Lester Thurow	MIT Economics Prof: *Computers and National Productivity*. An overview and analysis.	212
	Museum	3/10/89	Regis McKenna	Silicon Valley marketing wizard: *Who's Afraid of Big Blue?*	208
Artificial Intelligence	Harvard IT Series	2/28/89	Michael Arbib	Dir. USC Center for Neural Engineering: *Building Computers with "Intelligence"*.	207
	Museum	10/6/85	Richard Greenblatt	MIT Prof: *History of Artificial Intelligence at MIT and Xerox PARC*	195
Computer Systems	BCS-GM	12/21/88	Scott Fisher	NASA Project Director: *Virtual Environment Workstation*, What is it, why and how was it developed?	203
	BCS-GM	4/26/89	Dan Goldman	V.P. Digitalk: *Demystifying Object Oriented Programming: Smalltalk Language*.	209 209V
	BCS-GM	9/27/89	Didier Diaz	Project Manager presents, explains and demonstrates Apple's new *Macintosh Portable*.	218 218V
	BCS-GM	11/29/89	Stav Prodromou	Poqet founder presents pocket sized *Poqet Computer.* Runs for 100 hours on 2 AA batteries.	221 221V
	BCS-GM	2/28/90	Gene Banman and others	Sun Microsystems team demonstrates *"4th Wave Computing": SPARCStation 1*.	224 224V
	BCS-GM	5/23/90	Walt Simpson, David Jones	CEOs of Commodore and GoldDisk: *Amiga 3000 + Showmaker = Desktop Video.*	227 227V
	BCS-GM	1/23/91	Jerry Kaplan, Dan Bricklin	Co-founder Go Corp. and V.P. Slate Corp.: *Pen Based Computing: Concepts and Demonstration*.	229
	BCS-IBM	6/10/91	Bill Gates	Co-founder Microsoft: *The Future of Operating Systems and the Introduction of DOS 5.0*.	230
Software: The Creator's Perspective	BCS-GM	5/28/86	David Intersimone	V.P. Borland International: *Turbo Prolog* (*Byte*'s Bruce Webster gives rave notice); *Turbo Lightening*.	231
	BCS-GM	1/25/89	Mark Epply	CEO Traveling Software: *Sharp's coat pocket computer*. A precursor of the iPhone?	205
	BCS-GM	2/22/89	Frank King, Bill Gross	V.P. Lotus and Project Leader present and demonstrate data navigator *Magellan*.	206
	BCS-GM	5/24/89	Fred Wang	CEO Wang Labs: *Freestyle*. A superset of Wang's word processing system.	211
	BCS-GM	6/28/89	Donald R. Emery	CEO Reference Software: Grammatik III. New grammar checker. SIGGRAPH preview follows Q&A	216 216V
	BCS-GM	1/24/90	Jim Manzi	CEO Lotus and team: *Lotus 123G*. The graphical veersion of a software classic. Bob Frankston opens.	223 223V
	BCS-PC	10/6/88	Ed Esber	CEO Ashton-Tate: *Ashton-Tate's Long Range Database Strategy*. Incl. observations re user groups.	201
	BCS-PC	6/1/89	Philippe Kahn, R. Dickerson	Founder, Borland International & Proj.Mgr: *Turbo Pascal 5.5 and Reflex*. Also PK's overview of OOP.	214

Note: A "V" in the Pgm. No. column indicates that Powersharing has produced this "Evening with the BCS" as a video program as well as a narrated audio program.

Narrated Graphics and Powersharing's 10 Video Programs

Projected images featured in many BCS presentations and producer Mann narrated these as needed for an audio audience. In 1989, his assignment as Food Security Advisor to the Government of Malawi required increased travel. So that he could narrate as needed in producing the programs he missed, and also to produce some programs in both audio and video, he contracted with videographer Glenn Koenig to record the BCS presentations he missed. These were among the source tapes for the 42 unproduced programs he stored when he moved to Africa in 1991. For the new digital Series, Mann produced these 10 as both narrated audio and video programs. *At left, BCS President Rotenberg and visionary financier Ben Rosen: Pgm.#114.*

PROGRAMS PRODUCED 2015-2019

Category	Forum	Date	Speaker	Program Title and Information	Pgm. No.
Education and Games	BCS-GM	8/22/90	S.Arnold, D.Glenn,T.Gramani	*Lucas Arts Presents!* Interactive games; THX - sound stage audio quality for home theatres.	228 228V
	BCS-SI	6/7/89	Ronnie Rosenberg	MIT Ph.D.: *Euphoria about Computers in Schools is Unjustified*.	215
	Museum	10/24/85	Trip Hawkins	Founder, Electronic Arts: *The Rebirth of Home Computing*. New Amiga illustrates.	197
Oral History: The Pioneers	BCS-GM	3/28/90	Alvy Ray Smith	Co-Founder of Pixar: *Renderman and Desktop Visualization*. (Illustrated with 10 Pixar shorts.)	225 225V
	BCS-GM & NeXT	11/28/90	Steve Jobs and Pito Salas	NeXT founder Jobs says: *Lotus Improv on NeXT* "is the neatest program I have ever seen in my life".	200
	BCS-PC	5/4/89	Bill Gates	Co-founder Microsoft: Freewheeling presentation and discussion w BCS members.	210
	Museum	5/3/85	Dr. Koji Kobayashi	Leader of NEC of Japan: *The Development of the Japanese Computer Industry*.	193
	Museum	12/4/86	William Norris	CEO, Control Data Corp.: *Entrepreneurship, Cooperation and Computers*.	199
Communications and Networking	BCS-SI	10/19/88	Michael Lawson	*The Dukakis Campaign's use of Computer Communication*. (Now known as social media).	204
	BCS-SI	2/15/89	BCS Panel	*Computer Viruses*. An insightful discussion of the threat to computer security.	213
	BCS-GM	3/22/89	David Wax	*IBM+Sears = Prodigy*. GUI interface bundled on IBM PCs and compatibles. Challenges CompuServe.	233
	BCS-GM	10/25/89	Nat Goldhaber	Serial entrepreneur: *Computer Networking; Implications for Society*.	220
	BCS-GM	4/25/90	David Bunnell	Publisher (*PCWorld*, *Macworld*, etc.): *Bioworld*. Online information for the biotech industry.	226 226V
Own Business	BCS-C&E	10/00/90	BCS Panel	Consultants & Entrepreneurs Group presents: *Home Businesses: Challenges, Opportunities*.	219
International	BCS-SI	4/24/85	Janice Brodman	Harvard Researcher: *Microcomputers in the Third World: Implications for Women*.	202
	BCS-SI	10/6/86	Alex Randall leads Panel	*Computers in China*. First-hand reports, well-informed discussion.	232
	HIID	2/4/85	Janice Brodman	Harvard Researcher: *Microcomputers in the Third World: Boon or Boondoggle?*	198

Note: *A "V" in the Pgm. No. column indicates that Powersharing has produced this "Evening with the BCS" as both a video program and as a narrated audio program.*

Early BCS video recordings

Dan Bricklin, co-creator of VisiCalc and BCS Board Member, arranged for VisiCalc's parent firm to videotape and archive many early BCS presentations. The taping ended when VisiCalc was overwhelmed by Lotus 1-2-3. In 1985 VisiCalc was purchased and discontinued by Lotus Development Corp. Jonathan Rotenberg and Dan Bricklin are working with the Computer History Museum to produce and publish online these earlier BCS videos.

The Powersharing Series program #104 is Dan's tale of VisiCalc's rise and fall.

About the Drawings

Since Powersharing's founding in 1982, the drawings of fine artist Ann Leggett have helped to capture the theme of people sharing knowledge though these recordings. As Robert Tinney's BYTE covers wonderfully illustrate the technology itself, Ann's work highlights the users of the technology, imagining how they might use this Series. Ann has exhibited at galleries and institutions nation-wide, including the National Arts Club in New York, Princeton and Columbia Universities and Grand Central Galleries in NY. As a back-up trade, she trained as a long-haul truck driver, and in 1978-79, she piloted 18-wheelers cross-country, an experience that led to a splendid series of works inspired by the working people and places of the great American Road.

Ann Leggett's
self-portrait, drawn for
The Powersharing Series

From Ann's Letterhead

A review of the Series in
CHOICE: Current Reviews for College Libraries
The American Library Association, September 1987

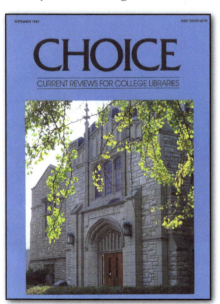

THE POWERSHARING SERIES: People, computers and you - ed. by Charles K. Mann.
Dist. by Powersharing, 152 Lockwood Rd., Riverside, CT 06878, 1986 (c1985).

A collection of 32 audiotapes of speeches and talks by computer pioneers, leaders, and professionals such as Steve Wozniak and Seymour Papert explaining particular components of computer use. Most of the presentations are speeches made at conventions and society meetings and consist of the presentation followed by a question-answer session with most running approximately 70 minutes long. General categories include information management, artificial intelligence, and education. Editor Mann has been very selective in the talks chosen and the individual talks have been supplemented with additional "low key" commentary to keep listening audiences in the picture. The sound is of high quality, having been recorded with the Dolby process. The resource guide that is attached is highly readable and informative. Each tape includes an overview and a discussion of how the content affects business, education, and the independent learner. The forum, time, and date are given for each. A unique and very useful resource for advanced undergraduate and graduate students in an independent learning situation.

-D.M. Moore, Virginia Polytechnic Institute and State University

Origin and Development of *The Powersharing Series*

Economist Charles Mann, a Rockefeller Foundation officer working on international food policy, was an early advocate of using "microcomputers" in international development projects. In 1982 he co-produced a video introduction to the Apple II and VisiCalc

Steve Wozniak and Series Editor Charles Mann with an Apple II computer at the Computer Museum, May 1986, following recording of *The Making of an Engineer and a Computer. The Powersharing Series* #133

titled *The Powersharing Series* featuring the co-founders of the Big Apple User Group, John and Barbara McMullen. In 1983 the BAUG and others hosted a Computer Fair with many industry pioneers. With such an "A List" all in one program, he underwrote professionally audio recording 30 of the sessions. He decided to produce 11 of these presentations as a continuation of the *The Powersharing Series.*

In 1985 he joined the Harvard Institute for International Development (HIID) where he continued to identify imaginative uses for PCs in development projects. With Prof. Steve Ruth he developed two books on the subject published by the American Association for the Advancement of Science. To bring the knowledge riches of user groups to a wider audience, he also expanded the Series, entering into formal recording agreements with both The Boston Computer Society and the Computer Museum.

When his economist career demanded ever more time and travel, he informed Gwen Bell, Director of the Computer Museum, that he could no longer continue the *Powersharing* recordings. She responded: "You can't stop. No one else will do what you are doing, and if you stop, these talks will be lost." A historian at heart, Mann continued underwriting and recording until, in 1991, Harvard sent him on a resident assignment to The Gambia in West Africa. He stopped all work on the *Series*, placing in long-term storage all of the equipment, tapes, and over 40 unproduced recordings.

When Mann retired from Harvard in 2002 he pursued his longstanding video interest, founding the Development Communications Workshop to mentor students in digital storytelling and produce educational films about international development. (Films are at: www.DER.org). In 2013 he returned to the unfinished *Powersharing Series* intent on producing a complete digital edition of all of the programs. With some support from the Computer History Museum which now holds all of Powersharing's recordings, in 2019 he published the completed Series on a 64GB flash drive, a format intended to make this resource readily available to libraries, schools, and universities.

The Powersharing Series CREDITS

The speakers whose wisdom and wit are the heart and soul of the *Series*;

Video series Co-Producer and Mann's multimedia mentor Martha Stuart;

NYC BAUG co-founders John and Barbara McMullen;

Audio Engineers: Bob Keil, Bonita Lei, John Cameron, Bruce Macomber;

Equipment and advice: AudioCom and Talamas Audio Services;

Videography: Glenn Koenig, Open Eyes Video;

Audiotape and videocassette conditioning: John Fede, Audio Video Recovery;

Graphic Designers: Ken Kleppert, Conrad Willeman, Bill Shea;

Attorneys: Grotta Glassman and Hoffman, Hemenway and Barnes;

Original Drawings: Ann Leggett;

Producer, Editor, Narrator: Charles Mann;

Audio Production Assistance: Dan Tritle and Brian Morris, Cape & Islands NPR;

Associate Editor for Digital Edition: Tom Frikker;

Special thanks: Jonathan Rotenberg, Gwen and Gordon Bell, Gardner Hendrie.

Copyrights and Trademarks

THE POWERSHARING

PEOPLE COMPUTERS AND YOU

SERIES ©

SPEND TIME WITH...

Seymour Papert, Steve Wozniak, Dan Bricklin, Steve Jobs, Ben Rosen, Bill Gates, Philippe Kahn, Jean-Louis Gassée, Patrick McGovern, Adam Osborne, Adam Green, Regis McKenna, Trip Hawkins, Howard Anderson, Philip Don Estridge, John Sculley, Mike Markkula, Mitch Kapor, Esther Dyson, Ray Kurzweil, Edward Feigenbaum, George Gilder, Marvin Minsky, Timothy Leary, Oliver Selfridge, Bill Machrone, Charlie Oppenheimer, Didier Diaz, Del Yocam, Stuart Alsop II, John Dvorak, Jerry Pournelle, Michelle Preston, Jim Seymour, Tom Rattigan, John Roach, Leonard Tramiel, Rod Canion, Bob Frankston, Jef Raskin, Tom Snyder, Bill Atkinson, Jim Manzi, David Ahl, Ken Arnold, Steve Russell, Dave Lebling, Chris Crawford, Tom Snyder, Dan Bunten, Erich Bloch, Walt Techner, Dennis Klatt, Bob Metcalfe, Bill Lowe, Michael Dell, Richard Stallman, William Norris, Ed Esber, David Bunnell, Alvy Ray Smith...

♪ WELCOME TO THE ♪ POWERSHARING ♪♪ SERIES

Powersharing Contact Information

For more information and contact details, please visit our website at www.*ThePowersharingSeries*.com